Solidity Sn

MW01290621

Build DApps In The Ethereum Blockchain

Introduction

I want to thank you and congratulate you for getting this book, "Solidity Smart Contracts: Build Dapps in the Ethereum Blockchain".

This book contains proven steps and strategies on how to become a master in solidity, smart contract creation and Ethereum blockchain development.

Hello and welcome to our course about smart contracts with Solidity.

In order to be able to start making your own smart contracts first, we need to take a step back and go through some of the most essential aspects of the Ethereum blockchain.

We will start with a little history about what exactly is the Ethereum blockchain and its part in this fast-growing global evolution in technology.

In order to understand the whole system and how to make our smart contract the best way possible with as fewer functionality costs, we need to go through the mechanics of the Ethereum blockchain.

I'll show you how to make your first wallet, how to manage it and from there we'll move on to a little cryptography, block analysis and gas prices.

Things might look a bit overwhelming at first but once you get the hang of it you'll appreciate that knowledge when we get to the coding part.

Every developer that makes smart contracts needs to have access to the test net network on which we will deploy our contracts. In order to do that we have to make a test net account alongside our main net one and most importantly we have to get some test net ether to work with.

I will show you a couple of easy ways to get as much ether as you might need, in your let's call it journey, into creating smart contracts with solidity.

We'll take a look at some block transactions and graph explanations. Some free to use but extremely helpful websites to help you track the blockchain network and much, much more.

Thanks again for buying this book, I hope you enjoy it!

What Is The Ethereum Blockchain?

In this first chapter, we're going to talk about the Ethereum blockchain and what it actually is.

During the past couple of years there's not many people that haven't heard at least a little about Bitcoins, Ethereum or the blockchain technology.

All the buzz generated by the media has led the industry to a giant leap and the best is yet to come.

I'll try to keep things as simple as possible and I won't go into non-essential stuff that might get you confused.

Ethereum by definition is an open-source public service that uses blockchain technology to aid smart contracts and cryptocurrency trading securely without a third party.

Ethereum offers two types of accounts: externally owned - those are the public accounts to which we own our private keys. Second ones are the contract accounts. Those are the accounts on which Ethereum developers deploy all kinds of smart contracts.

The Ethereum blockchain remains the biggest smart contract ecosystem being home to numerous alt coins and apps.

With its fast growing community and potential, a lot of big companies like JP Morgan, Intel and Microsoft are getting involved into the smart contract business and decentralized services.

Now we'll talk a little about the currency behind the Ethereum blockchain or the so-called ether.

That is the currency that we're going to use in our smart contract development with Solidity and it is the main currency that sponsors most of the ICOs.

By most predictions, it is expected that at some point in the not so far future it will even beat Bitcoin in market cap.

Being able to make your own smart contract not only gives you the ability to start a career in this fast growing industry, but it allows you to make your own DApp.

Some of the most famous ones are Crypto Kitties and IDEX.

The general idea, which the founder of Ethereum - Vitalik Buterin - had, was that the blockchain technology could do way beyond just payment transactions. So, at the age of 19 he released a white paper describing what would ultimately become Ethereum using a general scripting language.

The key difference from the mother coin - Bitcoin - was the platform's ability to trade more than just cryptocurrency.

Some of you might've heard about projects like Crypto Kitties, decentralized chats and all sort of other apps.

The thing is… blockchain technology is still evolving but everyone that has any interaction with it sees it is potential. The security behind every transaction is impenetrable because of the blockchain consensus algorithm.

In the next video I'm going to show you what blocks are, how are they generated and I'll show you the mechanics behind every operation that is being sent through the blockchain.

At last, we'll take a look at the current state of the blockchain, the problems that it faces and possible solutions.

Going More In Debth

In this chapter, we're going to talk about some technical but necessary things in the blockchain. Don't be scared… I'll keep things as simple as possible.

I am going to open a webpage called etherscan.io

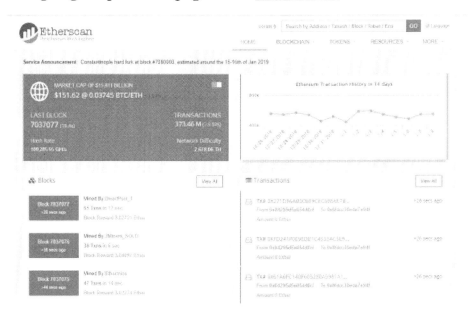

In this website, we can pretty much see every relevant statistic that we might need in order to track the blockchain movement.

First let us talk about how exactly information is being transmitted and stored on the blockchain.

If you have ever owned any kind of cryptocurrency, you would know that you have to pay some sort of transaction fee in order to send your money to someone else. That is not the same kind of fee that banks charge us when we make bank transfers but it is a fee to network itself.

Look at it this way…. When you hit "send", your transaction goes into a pool of other transactions that are waiting to be transmitted and validated by the network. And that validation, at least in the Ethereum blockchain, is being made by the so-called miners.

In order for a transaction to be made we have to tell the network how much gas money we're willing to pay. The higher the amount is, the faster our transaction will get into the next block that will be mined / validated.

We'll talk about gas in next lectures so for now just keep in mind that there is some kind of transaction fee.

Now let's take a look at Etherscan and what we can see.

On the left side there's a list with all recently generated blocks that have been validated by the network. Each of this blocks contains a number of transactions or smart contract operations.

Currently there's a new block every 14 seconds or so… which means that when you try to send currency to someone for instance your transaction will get into one of these blocks depending on the network traffic and the amount that you have set for gas money.

When we click on one of the generated blocks we'll see all the information that it holds.

First we have the height which is like the serial number of the block.

We have a time stamp to know when exactly it has been validated.

We can see the number of transactions that made it inside the block and if there are any… the number of internal smart contract transactions.

We're going to skip the hashes for now since there's no need to get into them at this point.

After that we can see who mined the block. Most of the times they're mined by pools which arc basically a collaboration between miners that split the price for each block they mine.

With time the difficulty of mining a block grows exponentially. Just for the past 10 months the difficulty has grown twice which means less profit for the miners.

After that we have the size of the block and all the information that it holds in bytes.

And beneath it is the used gas that people have paid for their transactions.

Every mined block has a fixed reward by the network of 3 ethers that goes to the address of the miner that has mined the block plus the gas money and uncles if there are some.

Uncles are so the so-called orphan blocks. Think of it this way …. One miner finds the correct block header and a second miner finds the solution a split second after him. The first miner keeps mining on the main blockchain while the second one is actually mining on a parallel one. When the next block comes after 14 seconds the two blockchain synchronize.

The difference between bitcoin uncles is that here the second miner is rewarded uncles for the amount of work that he has done during the blockchain was split.

Now let's click on the transactions and see what we have there:

In this window, we're getting information about all the transactions that are made it in the block.

We can see the unique hash for every single transaction. Sender's address and of course the receiver.

Also you can see the value that has been transferred.

You might notice that in some cases the value is zero ether. That is when the transaction is being made through a smart contract.

At the end we can see that transaction fee that is been paid for every single transaction.

The principle of the TxFees is kind of simple. According to the network speed and traffic we have N amount of transactions that can make it into the next block that is going to be mined. Whoever paid the biggest fee gets his transaction transmitted faster.

Paying the minimum doesn't mean your transaction won't be transmitted but it might take a little bit more time depending on the current traffic.

The problem with the Ethereum network (and not only) is that at least for now it is dependent on miners to validate blocks. And the problem with that is that mining equipment is extremely expensive and electricity consuming.

This is why for the past couple of years the team behind the Ethereum project and the community are taking steps to moving from POW (proof of work) to POS (proof of stake) validating mechanism. We will not be getting into them since they are not relevant to our course but if you are interested, there is tons of materials in the community about it.

The second and maybe bigger problem is the scaling of the network and increasing the TPS (transactions per second). Fortunately, with the fast growth of the community we might be seeing some big improvements in the near future.

In the next video, we'll be making our first Ethereum wallet and we'll go through all the necessary security instructions in order to keep our finances secure.

Get FREE Video Lessons on Solidity at codingsrc.com/solidity

Creating an Ether Wallet

In this video, we will be making our first Ethereum wallet, I will explain to you all the security risks and options that you have and hopefully you'll avoid getting hacked and losing your assets.

So first of all we need to go to https://www.myetherwallet.com/ .

When you open the webpage, you will see a popup with some information about the website. Personally, I suggest that you read it. It is kind of important.

Also make sure that every time when you open the website you see in the left side of the name bar "MyEtherWallet INC [US] ". If this is missing, you are most probably on a phishing site that wants to steal your info.

After you are done, the popup goes away and we are on the main page.

Here it is pretty much straight forward... you can see that in order to create our wallet the only thing that we are required to do is to type a password for it.

Before you type the password that you have in mind, be sure that it is something that you don't ordinary use on other websites, that is is a lot more complex and most importantly that you write it down on a piece of paper.

Now I'm going to type my password that I'll use in this course and click.

On the next window, we are asked to save our keystore file.

Save your **Keystore** File.

Download Keystore File (UTC / JSON)

"Do not lose it!" It cannot be recovered if you lose it.
"Do not share it!" Your funds will be stolen if you use this file on a malicious/phishing site.
"Make a backup!" Secure it like the millions of dollars it may one day be worth.

I understand. Continue.

In order to use your Ethereum wallet you are given a lot of ways to actually reach and unlock that wallet.

One of which is the keystore file. That file contains encrypted information about your personal private key with which you can unlock your wallet.

Download your file, save it on a flash drive and if it is possible make a backup of it on another drive. Never keep the file on your personal computer and never write your passwords on notes or any kind of files on your PC.

After we have downloaded the file click on continue.

Now the website provides us with our personal private key. This private key is unique, no one can see it during transactions and that is the key to all your digital assets.

You can copy/paste it in a folder inside the flash drive that you have used for the keystore file and also write it down on a piece of paper.

From here, the website takes us to the page that we're going to see every time we want to unlock and use our wallet.

As you can see, there is a lot of options but I am going to talk about the most common ones.

First, we have MetaMask / Mist. MetaMask is a browser extension that we're going to use a lot during the course. Because of which we'll have a separate video just for it.

Ledger is a hardware wallet. It is a device just like a flash drive with a software that protects your assets. It costs around 70-100 bucks depending on your country but it is by far the most secure way to protect your funds.

Trezor is the same hardware protection device but it is a bit larger... like an external hard drive.

We are skipping the next two and after that you can see we have the option to unlock our wallet with a keystore / JSON file.

When we click on that option you'll see that we're recommended not to use that option... why you ask? Well in order to use it we have to upload our file back to the server of the website and during that upload the file can be hijacked and eventually we might get hacked.

It is a good thing to save the file but try not to use it unless you have completely forgot and lost your password.

The next option is the mnemonic phrase. Think of it as an easy to remember unbreakable password. In different wallets / websites, the length is different but it is something between 14 and 21 words in a given order.

Again, the website tells us that it is not a recommended way to access our wallet. To be honest unless you have a hardware wallet it is never safe when you do it so always try to take the necessary precautions.

Like… **never** access your wallet from a public Wi-Fi, always check the website domain in case you have entered a phishing site by accident and stuff like that.

Last but not least, we have our private key option with the same recommendation. If you have clicked on the MetaMask option, you might have seen that it is the only option that is recommended for accessing your assets. That is why once we connect the extension to our wallet we don't need to go to the website or type any kind of information, which makes it safer.

I am going to enter the wallet with the JSON file since it is for teaching purposes only. As you can see after I have uploaded the file, I am asked to enter the wallet password as well.

No when we have unlocked it, we have access to all the information and assets inside.

On the first line, we have our address. That is the address to which everyone will send you Ethereum based currency.

We can re-download the JSON file and see our private key in case we have lost it.

We have an option to print a paper wallet, which I have never done to be honest, but it is another option for your security.

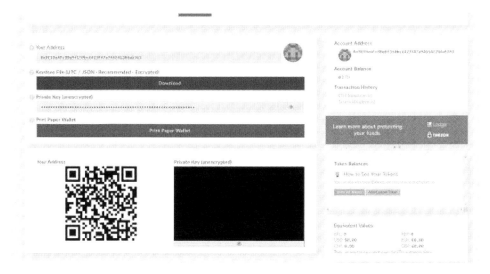

On the right side, you can see your current ETH balance. ETH is the main currency in our wallet. Beneath it, we have Token Balances.

That is where all Ethereum based tokens/coins will be shown. If you want to see all available tokens, press the "show all tokens" which will load a list with all of them.

In order to acquire a curtain type of token you need to find it in the list and click load. That way the token info will be uploaded to your wallet and you will be able to receive it.

Token Balances

How to See Your Tokens

You can also view your Balances on etherscan.io or ethplorer.io

Only Show Balances   Add Custom Token

Token Contract Address

mewtopia.eth

Token Symbol

Decimals

Save

Click to Load $FFC
Click to Load $FYX
Click to Load $HUR
Click to Load $IQN
Click to Load $TEAK

Last but not least, if you plan on investing in ICOs you will have to add the token info yourself.

You can do that by pressing the button for custom token in which you have to paste the token address, symbol and decimal that you have been given by the ICO.

Ok that was all about our first wallet creating and the most important things we need to know.

Get FREE Video Lessons on Solidity at codingsrc.com/solidity

Different Kinds of Wallets

So, in this video I will show you the different kinds of wallets that you can use.

For those of you that are familiar with them, feel free to skip this lesson and go straight to the next.

Ok… in the previous video we have made our first Ethereum wallet using the MyEtherWallet website. Those kinds of wallets are called online wallets. They should not be your first choice if you are a security freak or you have a big amount of money invested.

Let's talk about software wallets. One of the common software wallets is the official blockchain of the coin… for instance the Ethereum. But in order for your wallet to be functional you'll have to synchronize your copy of the blockchain with the official one which depending on the coin might take a lot of your hard drive and time.

I've personally used software wallets like Exodus: https://www.exodus.io/

It is an amazing application with pretty neat user interface that makes managing your assets easy and as secure as it can get on a software wallet. When you first download and install it you'll be given a mnemonic phrase of 14 words if I remember correctly.

Those 14 words are your backup key in case your PC gets broken, software gets deleted or any other kind of situation in which you lose control of your software. Of course, you'll be asked to type a password, which again I strongly suggest to be as unique and long as possible.

After that, we have the so-called hardware wallets. I've told you in the previous video about the Nano Ledger and Trezor devices … so let's see them now.

Here's the website of the Nano Ledger: https://www.ledger.com/

It looks like a flash drive but don't get fooled, the security behind it is amazing. Again, we have a mnemonic phrase, passcode and high standard of security. If you lose your ledger, you can always order a new one and put the coins from your lost one with the mnemonic phrase. The advantage of hardware wallets compared to the software wallets is that they are pretty much unhackable.

He's the website for the Trezor wallet: https://trezor.io/

As i told you before… it is pretty much the same device with different look.

And last but not least… we have exchange wallets.

During the past couple of years, a lot of exchanges got hacked and a lot of people lost most or all of their money, which led to big dumps to the prices of all cryptocurrencies.

But even after those things a lot of people are still using exchange accounts to store their assets. Don't get me wrong… if you someday decide to day trade it is fine but always have in mind not to keep big amounts of coins no matter how big or trusted the exchange is.

For the sake of the example I'll show you one of the biggest exchanges : https://www.binance.com/

The security measures are getting better and better every day so that people can feel safer trusting their assets to the exchanges. For instance after you make an account you'll notice that you have several layers of protection just to get inside of your account.

After that if you try to withdraw funds you'll have to verify the transaction by code sended to your phone or authenticator, email or whatever option you have added.

The most important thing about handling cryptocurrencies is that you acknowledge that you and only you take responsibility about what happens to your assets and where you trust them to be kept safe.

In the next video we'll talk about Metamask, I'll show you the difference between handling a main net and test net wallet and after that we'll take a look at what GAS is.

See you in the next lecture.

<u>Get FREE Video Lessons</u> <u>on Solidity at</u> <u>codingsrc.com/solidity</u>

Introduction to Metamask

Hi… In this video, I'm going to show you the main app that we'll be using as our wallet.

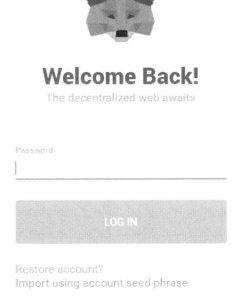

As I've said in the previous videos, Metamask has become essential when we want to get into the smart contract business.

So let's start by saying what Metamask actually is….

The application is actually a google chrome extension. It works with ERC-20 tokens, which are the most common ones in the Ethereum blockchain, and believe it or not, it is one of the most secure software wallets out there.

Let's start by installing the extension to our chrome browser.

Just type the name in the google store search bar and it should be the first one to pop out.

When we have added the Metamask to our browser, it is time to set it up.

First, we're going to make our first account. In order to do that we're asked to type a password and confirm it.

Again as in all other types of wallets, use something unique as password that you don't usually use on other websites and write it down on a piece of paper.

Now we're given a so-called "seed" or a mnemonic phrase. This phrase is our backup key.

If my PC gets broken, lost, or stolen and I need to reinstall Metamask on another device… that is the key that'll do the trick.

I strongly suggest that you don't save the "seed" on your PC or any kind of electronic device for that matter. Write it down on a piece of paper … at least 2-3 times and put the copies on a secure location.

Now… after we're done with the backup of our seed Metamask asks us to double check our seed and enter it in the system. This way we'll be 100% sure that we have wrote it down correctly and that it works.

And that is it… our account is all set up. Now we're getting to the more interesting part.

Let's first click on the Metamask icon and see what we have there….

As you can see our balance is currently zero.

On the top of the extension, we can see this little box that tells us on which network were currently connected to…

As any other developer, we need a safe place where we can test and deploy our work and at this case our smart contracts.

Now… Let's get out hands on some free ether that we send to our accounts in the test network.

First thing we need to do is to go to this website :
https://faucet.rinkeby.io/

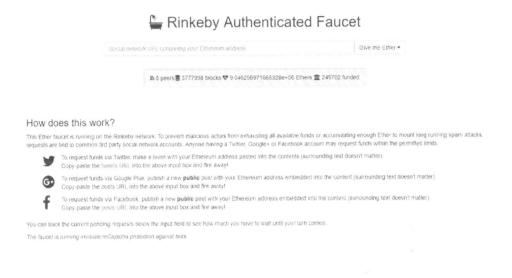

Here we're given three options that are basically time related so that it can prevent spamming of the service.

Let's go for the highest amount… so in order to get those 18.5 ethers all we have to do is go to our Metamask and click on "copy to clipboard" at our test net address.

After that, we just have to paste that address in any of the three Social Medias and copy/paste the link to the post back on Rinkeby website.

Everything takes about 1-2 minutes or less when you get the hang of it.

…and we are done.

We have 18.5 ethers to work with while we learn to make your first smart contracts with Solidity.

You might be asking why we need ether at all if we're going to make smart contracts…

Well as I've said in previous videos there's this thing called GAS that we all pay when we want to make a transaction or at our case for every operation that our smart contracts does.

So think of the GAS as the internal pricing for running a transaction or contract in the Ethereum network.

As I've said before, the higher amount of gas, you're willing to pay,

the faster your transaction will get into the next block...

With smart contracts, it gets a bit trickier since we spend gas for every line of code.

Here's a simple table that shows us some of the gas values per action:

Operation name	Gas Cost	Function
step	1	Default amount of gas to pay for an execution cycle.
stop	0	Nothing paid for the SUICIDE operation.
sha3	20	Paid for a SHA3 operation.
sload	20	Paid for a SLOAD operation.
sstore	100	Paid for a normal SSTORE operation (doubled or waived sometimes).
balance	20	Paid for a BALANCE operation
create	100	Paid for a CREATE operation
call	20	Paid for a CALL operation.
memory	1	Paid for every additional word when expanding memory
txdata	5	Paid for every byte of data or code for a transaction
transaction	500	Paid for every transaction

As you can see it might get pricey to deploy and run our smart contract so it is very important to do it right.

But don't get scared of the numbers... the actual price of 1 gas/ ether is a really small sum which depends on the current network traffic and the number of miners that are validating the transactions.

If we go back to https://etherscan.io/chart/gasprice the website that we have visited in one of our first videos we can see the current GAS price and also the min and max.

Now you might ask why it says that min GAS value is 1 wei.

Wei is the smallest denomination of ether.

1 ether is equal to 1,000,000,000,000,000,000 Wei (10^{18})

1 **quintillion. One with 18 zeroes**

If the gas price drops a lot, the min amount is counted in wei…

Before we move to your first lecture about smart contracts let's finish with restoring our Metamask account.

Right click on the icon and remove it from chrome.

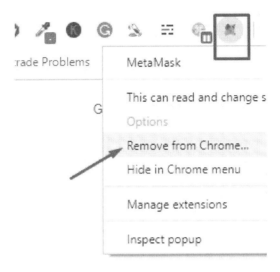

Now that we have removed it… which should play the broken PC scenario or any other kind of "disaster" …

let's go to the store and install it again.

Ok, we have it installed Metamask again

Now we have to accept all terms and conditions.

The first window after that is for restoring a previous wallet using the seed words that we have saved.

Type in your words in the correct order and a set a password.

We can restore the account using the seed but with every new installation, we have to set a new password.

And that is it.

Ok… I think that is all we need to know about Metamask and GAS.

So the next step is to start learning about solidity and smart contracts.

See you in the next lecture.

Introduction to Solidity: Contracts, Constructors and Functions

In this lecture, we are going to talk about **contracts, constructors and functions.**

OK, let's dive right in.

Let's first see what is the structure of a solidity source file.

Here we can see a sample contract.

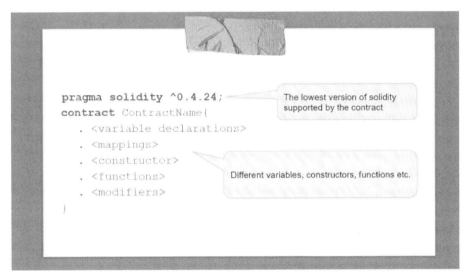

On the top of every solidity file there is the so-called version pragma, which tells us the lowest version of solidity supported by the contract.

After that, we have the contract and its name.

Inside it we can put variable declarations, mappings, constructors, functions, modifiers etc.

Now, let's see a sample contract.

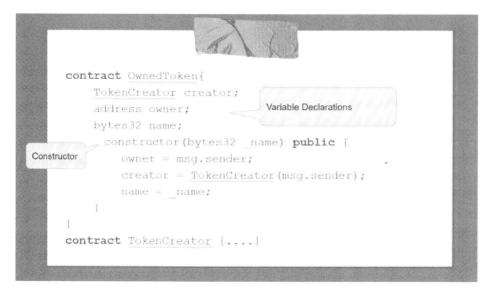

```
contract OwnedToken{
    TokenCreator creator;
    address owner;                    Variable Declarations
    bytes32 name;
    constructor(bytes32 _name) public {
        owner = msg.sender;
        creator = TokenCreator(msg.sender);
        name = _name;
    }
}
contract TokenCreator {....}
```

Here we have two contracts called **Owned Token** and **Token Creator**. You can have multiple contracts declared in one solidity file.

As you can see, we can also call contracts from other contracts as in this example.

After this, we have the variable declarations owner and name, which are used to store the address of the owner of the contract and the name of the contract.

Just below them, we have a constructor. Keep in mind that several versions before a constructor was declared as a function with the same name like the contract. However, now we use the keyword constructor.

So a constructor is a function that runs only once when the contract is deployed to a network.

When we deploy this contract, we can send the variable name with it. This variable is saved in the state variable name and our wallet address, from which we deployed the contract with, is saved in the state variable owner.

Now we can use this reference to check and restrict functions to be used by someone who is not the owner of the contract.

Ok, now let's see what is the structure of a function.

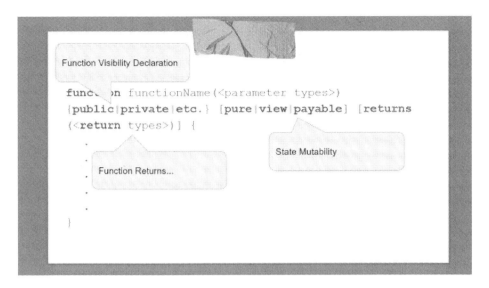

If you are familiar with JavaScript, functions look a lot like the ones there. However, we have some additional modifiers. After the function name and the variables that the function receives, we have visibility declaration, state mutability and the return types of the function.

For visibility, we can have public, private, internal and external. For the state mutability, we can have pure, view and payable. And in order to return some variables from a function at the end we should add the keyword 'returns' and in brackets the type of variables that we want to return. Here we can return more than one variable, so keep that in mind.

Ok, let's look at the different types of visibility in more detail. As we said, we have four different types of visibility - public, external, internal and private.

Those visibility declarations can be applied both to functions and to variables except for the external keyword, which is only for functions.

When we declare a function, the default visibility of it is public. We can call this function internally and externally and everyone has access to it.

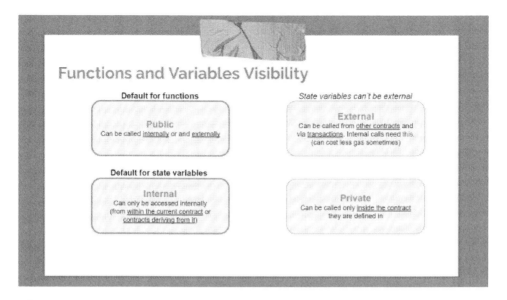

The external keyword works almost the same, however, when you try to call the function internally (from within the contract or another function in the contract) you will need to use the 'this.' in order to access it.

This might seem a little inconvenient. However, external functions can cost less gas sometimes, because sometimes they are more efficient when they receive large arrays of data.

We can also have internal functions that can only be accessed internally from the current contract or from contracts deriving from it.

Last but not least, we have private functions, which can be called ONLY from the contracts they are defined in. They are usable only internally in the same contract.

Now let's see an example of external and public functions.

Here we have a Sample contract.

EXTERNAL & PUBLIC FUNCTIONS

```solidity
pragma solidity^0.4.24;

contract SampleContract {
    unint256 external age; //ERROR: Can't use external for variables

    function test(uint[20] a) public pure returns (uint){
        return a[10]*2;
    }

    function test2(uint[20] a) external pure returns (uint){
        return a[10]*2;
    }
```

Uses less gas

```solidity
    function test3(uint[20] a) public view {
        this.test2(a);
    }
}
```

Will throw error if not using this.

At the first line as you can see I have declared a variable as external. If you try to do that, you will get an error and the contract will not compile. Remember - state variables do not have an external visibility.

However, here I have created public and external functions. Both of them do the same operation, but the external function will cost less gas in the end. External functions are more efficient when they receive large arrays of data so you can use them to make your contract more efficient.

And at the end I have declared a function in which I try to call the external function test2. However, I needed specify it as this.test2() in order to access the external function internally.

So remember if you want to call external functions internally, you need to add the keyword this. In front of the function.

Now, let's look at an example of internal and private functions.

INTERNAL & PRIVATE FUNCTIONS

```solidity
// This will not compile

pragma solidity ^0.4.0;

contract C {
    uint private data;

    function f(uint a) private returns(uint b) { return a + 1; }
    function setData(uint a) public { data = a; }
    function getData() public returns(uint) { return data; }
    function compute(uint a, uint b) internal returns (uint) { return a+b; }
}

contract D {
    function readData() public {
        C c = new C();
        uint local = c.f(7); // error: member "f" is not visible
        c.setData();
        local = c.getData();
        local = c.compute(3, 5); // error: member "compute" is not visible
    }
}

contract E is C {
    function g() public {
        C c = new C();
        uint val = compute(3, 5); // access to internal member (from derived to parent contract)
    }
}
```

Here we have 3 contracts C, D and E.

Contract C has one private function, two public functions and an internal function called compute.

In contract D if we try to call the function f of the contract C we are going to get an error because the function is declared private and is visible only inside the contract that it is defined in.

Also if we try to call the function compute from contract D we are also going to get an error because contract D is not derivative of contract C.

However, contract E is derivative of C. We declare this with the keyword 'is' as you can see in the example. If you have any prior programming knowledge this is called inheritance.

Because, our contract is derivative of contract C we can now call the the compute function as it is internal member.

Now, let's talk about the state mutability of function.

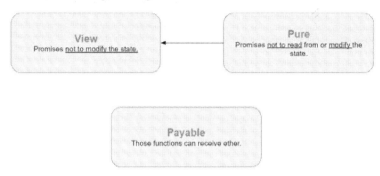

We have three different modifiers for that.

We have view, pure and payable.

If we declare a function to be a view function we basically promise not to modify the state.

Pure functions are derivatives of view functions. However, pure functions promise not only not to modify the state, but also not to read from state.In the next slides we will see more specific restrictions to those functions.

The last state mutability we can have is payable. Basically, the functions that are annotated with this modifier can receive ether and can make operations with those ethers.

Now, let's look at some examples.

Here is an example of a view function that you can create:

VIEW FUNCTIONS

```solidity
pragma solidity ^0.4.24;

contract C {
    function f(uint a, uint b) public view
returns (uint) {
        return a * (b + 42) + now;
    }
}
```

This function takes two variables "a" and "b" and returns "a" times (b + 42) + now.

Now is a global variable that gives you the time now as a timestamp variable.

When you have a view function, you CAN NOT write to state variables, emit events, send ether, call functions that are not pure or view, etc. I have listed the things that are not allowed in view functions on the right side here.

Now... Pure functions have the same restrictions as view functions as well as that they can't read form state variables...

PURE FUNCTIONS

```solidity
pragma solidity ^0.4.16;

contract SampleContract {

    function func1(uint x, uint y) private pure returns (uint) {
        return x * (y + 42);
    }

    function func2(uint a) private pure returns (uint b) {
        return a + 1;
    }

    function func2() public pure returns (string) {
        return "You are AWESOME!";
    }
}
```

In this example, we have three pure functions. The first two functions take variables x and y and do some mathematical operations and return the result. The third one just returns a string of "You are AWESOME!". Those are some perfect examples of pure functions that you can use.

However, there are some additional restrictions that you should keep in mind like that you can't access this.balance, <address>.balance, blocks, tx, msg variables or call functions that are not marked as pure.

Now let's see an example of a payable function:

In order to receive Ether you need to provide the 'payable' keyword to a function, otherwise the function will reject all Ether send to it.

In this example contract we have a public declared variable amount of 0 and we have a payable function pay me. The variable msg.value gives the amount of ether that was send to the function and adds it to the variable amount.

This is the basics of the tokens created on the Ethereum blockchain. In reality, it is a little bit more complicated but the fundamentals are the same. So let's stop here and have some practice lesson in our next lecture.

Get FREE Video Lessons on Solidity at codingsrc.com/solidity

What Is Remix And How To Use It?

Ok, so in this lecture we are going to take a brief look at the online IDE that we can use to make our solidity contracts and test them fast.

So, you need to open remix.ethereum.org

Here we can see a sample contract that is already written out for us to test out.

However, we are going to write our own contract to start out.

Now I would want from you to click on the plus sign here on the top left hand side of the website.

Give whatever name you like for the solidity file. I will name mine **Messenger**.

As we discussed in the previous lecture on top of every solidity file we need the so-called version pragma. So type '**pragma solidity ^0.4.24**';

```solidity
pragma solidity ^0.4.24;

contract Messenger{
    address owner;
    string[] messages;

    constructor() public {
        owner = msg.sender;
    }

    function add(string newMessage) public {
        require(msg.sender == owner);
        messages.push(newMessage);
    }

    function count() view public returns(uint){
        return messages.length;
    }

    function getMessages(uint index) view public returns(string){
        return messages[index];
    }
}
```

This is the latest solidity so far.

In addition, just below that we are going to define our contract. Type **contract Messenger** and curly brackets.

On the first line, we are going to define a variable address called owner. In the next lecture, we are going to talk more about variables, so just bear with me here.

So, we type address private owner;

On the next line, we are going to define an array of strings called messages.

Just below our declared variables, we are going to define a constructor.

Type **constructor** opened and closed brackets, public and opened and closed curly brackets.

Inside the curly brackets, we are going to type **owner = msg.sender.**

This line will define the owner as the person who has deployed the contract.

On the next line we are going to define a function add with input variables of a string called **newMessage**.

The visibility will be public and we will open and close curly brackets.

Inside the brackets, we are going to type the following

require (msg.sender == owner);

This line will prevent anyone who is not the owner of the contract to add messages to the array messages.

We are going to talk about this in more detail in the following lectures.

Just below this we are going to type
messages.push(newMessage);

This line will add a new message to the array of messages.

Below that we are going to define a function called **count** which is a view public function and returns a **uint**.

Inside the curly brackets, we are going to return **messages.length**, which will return the number of messages inside the array.

Below this, we are going to define one last function called **getMessage** that is going to take a variable **uint** called **index**.

The function will be **a view public function** and it will return a **string**.

Inside of the function, we are going to return the message with the index we give to the function.

Ok so now we are ready to compile our contract and deploy it to a virtual network.

We need to click here on the compile tap and the on start to compile.

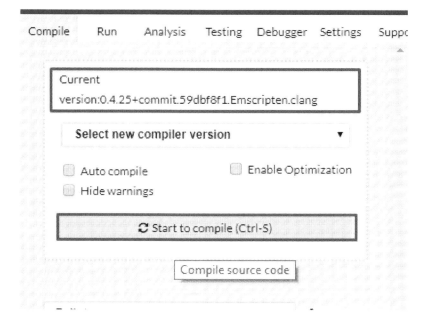

We get a Messenger in green, which means that we have no errors in our code.

If you have any errors or warnings, you will see here some notifications in yellow or red.

They are very explicit in what the error is so you can correct it.

Ok now we can go on the Run tab over here.

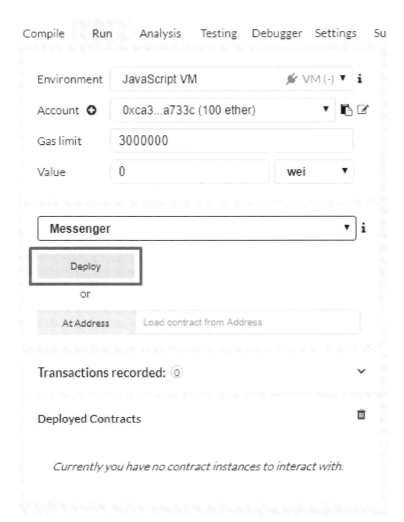

Here on the top we have a drop down menu called environment.

We have 3 choices - JavaScript VM, Injected Web3 and Web3 Provider.

We are going to choose JavaScript Virtual Machine.

Below this, we have 5 virtual Ethereum wallets. After that, the gas limit for the transactions and blow that the Ethereum in **weis** that we want to send to a function.

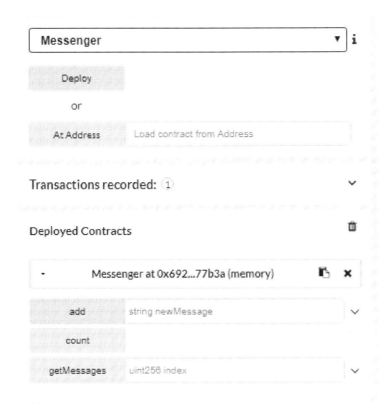

Below this, we have a drop down of the contracts that we have in the solidity file. For now, we have only one contract called messages so we select this.

And… we click **deploy**.

Now here we can see that we have deployed our contract successfully and we have access to the following functions - **add, count** and **getMessage**

In the debugger console over here, you can see some more details about the deployment.

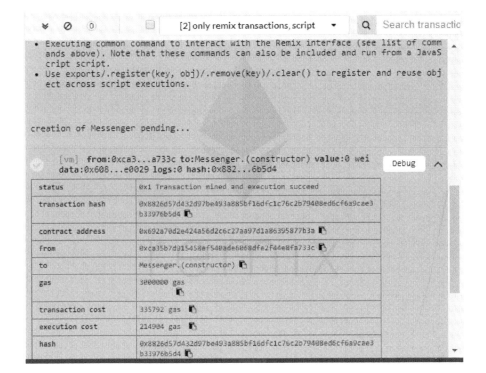

You can see the status of the transaction is success

You can see the contract address and who deployed the contract and other details about the gas and input.

Ok so now let's try to add a message to our messenger.

Let's type here "first message" in quotes. Don't forget to add the quotes otherwise you will get an error. This is just how string inputs are typed here.

Now let's click on the add button and see what happens.

As you can see, the transaction was a success.

We gave this input to the function **Messenger.add**

Now let's check on the count.

We have one message in our Messenger.

Now let's try to return this message.

Type **0** in the **getMessage** function and hit on the button.

Here you can see we had a call function, which gave us an output of the **"new message"**

However if we try to return an index that doesn't exist we are going to get an error.

Let's try typing **1** and pressing on **getMessage**.

Here you can see that we get an **error of invalid opcode.**

I want to show you one more thing.

Remember that we restricted the add function to be usable only to the contract owner, here?

Now let's change the account to another one and try to add a message.

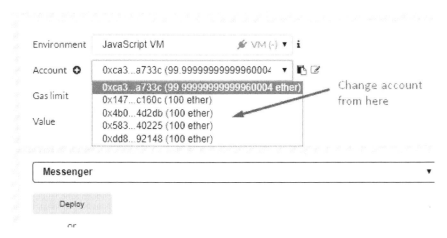

Let's type "test message" in quotes and hit on the add button.

As you can see we get an error, **revert**. The transaction stopped here and did not let us push the message to the messenger because we are not the owners.

Ok so now you have created your new contract and you got familiar with the Remix IDE a little bit.

Now let's continue with our lectures and get more in depth with solidity.

UPDATE: For anyone who wants to use this in the newer version of **solidity ^0.5.1** use the code below. The difference is that we need to specify that our strings are memory variables explicitly:

```solidity
pragma solidity ^0.5.1;

contract Messenger{
    address owner;
    string[] messages;

    constructor() public {
        owner = msg.sender;
    }

    function add(string memory newMessage) public {
        require(msg.sender == owner);
        messages.push(newMessage);
    }

    function count() view public returns(uint){
        return messages.length;
    }

    function getMessages(uint index) view public returns(string memory){
        return messages[index];
    }
}
```

Get FREE Video Lessons on Solidity at codingsrc.com/solidity

Variables in Solidity

Ok, now in this video we are going to talk about the different variables in solidity.

Solidity is a statically typed language, which means that the type of each variable needs to be specified

The most important value types that you should remember are - bool, integers, address, bytes, string, hex and enum

Variables:

→ Bool
True or false

→ Integers
Int8-int256 / uint8-uint256

→ Fixed numbers (to be added)

→ Address

→ Bytes

→ String, Hex and Enum
Provide a simple unifying message for what is to come

Booleans, as you may know, are data types that may have only two possible values - true or false. In Solidity, we define them with the keyword bool.

The integers in solidity however are a little bit more interesting.

If you don't know, an integer is a number with no fractional part; it can be positive, negative or zero.

Here they are defined in bits from 8 to 256 and can be signed or unsigned.

Signed can have positive and negative value.

As for unsigned they are only positive numbers inside.

In solidity, we don't have decimal or floating numbers for now.

Fixed-point numbers are defined in the documentation as a way to define decimal numbers, however, with a big warning sign that says that they are not fully supported yet. So, for now we don't have decimal values but keep in mind that in the future this might change.

Now... the address type holds a 20-byte value, which is the size of an Ethereum address.

Addresses also have members and serve as a base for all contracts.

We also have string types, which are written with either double or single-quotes and can hold text. Hex types hold hexadecimal strings, and enum values are one way to create user-defined types in Solidity.

Now let's see the Integer types in more detail:

int8	-128 to 127	uint8	0 to 127
int16	-32,768 to 32,767	uint16	0 to 32,767
int32	-2,147,483,648 to 2,147,483,647	uint32	0 to 2,147,483,647
...	...	...	...
int256	−115792089237316195423570985008 6879078532699846656405640394575 84007913129639935 to 115792089237316195423570985008 6879078532699846656405640394575 84007913129639935	uint256	0 to 115792089237316195423570 9850086879078532699846656 4056403945758400791312963 9935

Comparisons: <=, <, ==, !=, >=, > (evaluate to bool)

Bit operators: &, |, ^ (bitwise exclusive or), ~ (bitwise negation)

Arithmetic operators: +, -, unary -, unary +, *, /, % (remainder), ** (exponentiation), << (left shift), >> (right shift)

Integers, as I said, can be signed and unsigned.

Signed integers are defined with the keyword **int** and unsigned - with the keyword **uint**.

The integers are defined in bits and go from 8 to 256 and are in steps of 8.

Here in this table you can see the minimum and maximum values.

Keep in mind that if you define integers without the numbers at the end, only with **uint** or **int**, those are aliases for uint256 and int256, respectively.

You are responsible for best optimizing your code so use the corresponding size according to your needs. It is your own decision whether to use uint8 or uint256 (or whatever size) depending how big or small you expect the number in question to be.

So...with integers you can do comparison, bit and arithmetic operations as listed below this table.

Just keep in mind that as in other programming languages you can have overflow or underflow of a number. For example if you define a uint256 equal to 0 and then you subtract 1 from that number you will get this large number over here.

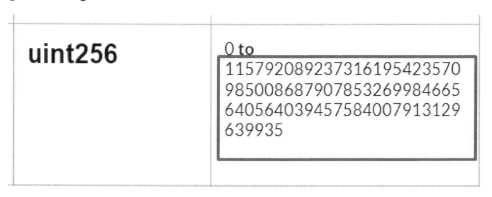

| uint256 | 0 to 115792089237316195423570985008687907853269984665640564039457584007913129639935 |

This can cause you a lot of trouble so be aware of it.

The next variable that we are going to discuss is the address variable. Addresses are the Ethereum addresses.

For each address variable, we have the following members.

We have balance, which gives us the balance of the address in wei.

We have transfer that can send a given amount of wei to an address.

We have send that does the same. However, the difference here is that transfer throws if it fails and send returns false if it fails. Otherwise, both do the same thing.

We have also call, call code and delegate call, which are low-level calls.

We are going to skip on what those address members do for the moment, but just keep in mind that they exist.

Bytes

[bytes1, bytes2, bytes3, ..., bytes32]   byte is an alias for bytes1.

Bytes are the binary representation of data.

Cheaper than saving data as strings

We also have bytes, which are the binary representation of data.

As you can see, we can have fixed size bytes from byte1 to byte32.

They store from 1 to 32 bits of data inside respectively.

We would want to use bytes over strings whenever we want to optimize our contracts to be cost efficient.

Usually working with strings instead of bytes will take up a little bit more gas when running a function.

Second reason to use bytes over string is smart-contract-to-smart-contract relations. Solidity is still unable to return string as function result for other contracts.

It may look like really unnecessary stuff to know, but smart contracts are getting complex with each day and the further it goes, the more contract to contract relations are going to appear on Blockchain.

And last we are going to see the strings, hex and enums.

String, Hex and Enum

Strings are written with either double or single-quotes ("foo" or 'bar')

Hexadecimal Literals are prefixed with the keyword hex and are enclosed in double or single-quotes (hex"001122FF")

Enums are one way to create a user-defined type in Solidity:

```
enum ActionChoices { GoLeft, GoRight, GoStraight, SitStill }
```

Strings are sequence of characters that are written with either double or single-quotes like in this example.

Hexadecimal Literals are prefixed with the keyword hex, are enclosed in double or single-quotes, and are saved in byte variables.

And last there are enums which are user-defined types in solidity. As you can see in this example, you can create enum called Action Choices with Go Left, Go Right, Go Straight and Sit still. You should always use enums when a variable (especially a method parameter) can only take one out of a small set of possible values like in this example.

Ok so now we know the basic types in Solidity. Let's continue to the next lecture to have some practice in remix again.

REMIX PRACTICE: Variables

In this lecture, we are going to have some practice in remix with variables.

Let's open remix and create a new solidity file.

Let's name it Variable Examples and press enter.

On top as always, we need to put the version pragma.

So type **pragma solidity ^0.4.24;**

After that create our contract named **VariableExamples.**

Now let's define some variables.

Type **bool switchedOn = true;**

Below this type address **owner = msg.sender;**

After that **uint8 number = 8;**

Below it a **bytes32** variable called **awesom1 = "Solidity is Awesome!"**

And right after it a **string** variable called **awesome2** with the same text;

```
1   pragma solidity ^0.4.24;
2
3 ▾ contract VariableExamples {
4       bool switchedOn = true;
5       address owner = msg.sender;
6       uint8 number = 8;
7       bytes32 awesome1 = "Solidity is awesome!";
8       string awesome2 = "Solidity is awesome!";
9   }
```

Now let's compile and deploy our contract.

Click on the compile after that go to run and deploy.

Hmm… We have successfully deployed our contract. However, we cannot see the variables and interact with them in any way whatsoever.

If you remember in the previous lectures, I told you that we can put visibility to variables as well as on functions.

The default visibility, when we declare a variable is internal.

This means that the variables are accessible only internally inside the contract and its derivative contracts.

So let's change the variables to public and see what happens.

```
pragma solidity ^0.4.24;

contract VariableExamples{
    bool public switchedOn = true;
    address public owner = msg.sender;
    uint8 public number = 8;
    bytes32 public awesome1 = "Solidity is awesome!";
    string public awesome2 = "Solidity is awesome!";
}
```

Type public here for every variable and then recompile the contract.

Now before we deploy it lets delete the previous instance and then redeploy the contract.

As you can see now we can see all the variables are accessible and we can return the values.

Remember when I said in the previous lecture that bytes are more cost effective then string values.

Well let's see how much gas does it cost calling the string and calling the byte variables.

As you can see the byte variable costs less gas then the string.

Now that you have seen this let me show you one of the traps that you can fall with integers.

Let's create a new file called **OverflowAndUnderflow**.

On top of the file, let's specify our version pragma.

After that, let's create the contract.

```solidity
pragma solidity ^0.4.24;
contract OverflowAndUnderflow {
    function overflow() public pure returns(uint256){
        uint256 max = 2**256-1;
        return max +1;
    }

    function underflow() public pure returns(uint256){
        uint256 min = 0;
        return min-1;
    }
}
```

Inside we will specify a function called **overflow**.

The function will be a **public pure function**…and it will return a **uint256**.

Inside we will declare a variable **uint256** called **max** equal to **2 to the power of 256 minus 1**.

In Solidity, using **double stars** like that will raise the number to the power of another number.

This will give us the maximum value of the uint256.

If we then **return max + 1** let's see what we will get.

Let's compile the contract and deploy it.

Now let's call the function overflow and see what we get.

We get the value of **0**.

The same goes the other way around which is called **underflow**.

Let's copy this function, change its name to underflow, and delete everything inside.

Let's create a **uint256** called **min equal to zero.**

And right below it **return min minus 1**;

Let's recompile the contract again

After that go to the run tab and first delete the previous contract.

Now deploy the contract again.

Let's click on the underflow function and see what we get.

We get the maximum value of the **uint**.

This is one of the most important things that you should remember about integers in solidity because that can cause you a lot of trouble.

And after all we are working with money and we need to be sure that whenever we do some mathematical operations we will not overflow or underflow our variable.

Ok so now we saw how we can expose our variables inside a contract and the dangers of integer variables.

Let's continue with our lectures in the next video.

Get FREE Video Lessons on Solidity at codingsrc.com/solidity

Getters and Setters

In this lecture, we are going to talk about getters and setters in solidity.

If you haven't heard of getters and setters before here is the definition

A getter is a function that gets the value of a specific property. A setter is a function that sets the value of a property

Let's see an example of a getter function.

```
contract SampleContract{
    uint256 public publicNumber;
    uint8 private secretNumber;
    function getSecret() view public returns(uint8){
      return secretNumber;
    }
}
```

H
ere you can see a sample contract with two numbers - public number and secret number.

The first number is with visibility public and the second is with private.

As I showed you in the previous lecture public variables get automatically a getter function, so if you want to access a variable as it is you can just make it public.

You can also make a function like this called **getSecret**, which needs to be public of course, that can return you private or internal variables and expose them.

Now let's see an example of a setter.

Here we have a Message Contract with a private variable message, a getter and a setter.

```
contract MessageContract{
    string private message = "Hello World";

    function getMessage() public constant returns(string){
      return message;
    }

    function setMessage(string newMessage) public {
      message = newMessage;
    }
}
```

With the setter, you can change the value of the private variable to whatever you want.

Now let's go in Remix and see the getters and setters in action.

Let's create a new file called **GettersAndSetter** and press enter.

On top as always, type the **version pragma.**

Let's copy and paste the **MessageContract** from the presentation and see how it works.

Now compile the contract and deploy it.

We have the two functions available over here - getMessage and setMessage.

If we click on the **getMessage** we will get the "Hello World" message that was predefined.

Let's try to change that with the setter.

Type in quotes "Changed Message" and click on **setMessage**.

The function was successfully executed.

Now let's see if we have changed the value of the message.

Click on getMessage again and as you can see, we have changed its value.

Now you know how getters and setters work in solidity.

Let's continue to the next lecture and go more in depth with Solidity

Arrays

In this lecture, we are going to talk about arrays.

If you don't know what arrays are, they are a series of objects all of which are the same size and type. Each object in an array is called an array element.

For example, you could have an array of integers, strings, bytes etc.

To define an array you should type the variable type and square brackets after it.

You access an element of an array with its sequential positions starting from 0. For example, the third element of an array will be the array name and number 2 in square brackets.

Arrays can have a fixed size or they can be dynamic.

FIXED SIZE ARRAYS

```solidity
pragma solidity^0.4.24;

contract SampleContract {
    uint8[3] nums = [10, 20, 30];

    function getNums() public returns (uint8[3]){
        nums[0] = 11;
        nums[1] = 22;
        nums[2] = 33;
        return nums;
    }

    function getLength() view public returns (uint){
        return nums.length;
    }
}
```

0	1	
10	20	

Will change the numbers

Returns the size of the array

Here we have an example of a fixed size array.

We have a Sample Contract with an array of fixed size of 3 called **nums**.

Inside the array, we have predefined the numbers 10, 20 and 30.

Below this, we have a function called getNums, which would return the array

However, before we return it we want to change the values.

Here on the first place we will put the number 11.

The second number we substitute with 22 and the third with 33.

After that, we return the array with its new numbers inside.

At the end, we have a function get length that will return the number of elements in the array.

Now let's look at an example of a dynamic array and what we have there.

To define a dynamic array you should leave the square brackets empty.

DYNAMIC ARRAYS

```solidity
pragma solidity^0.4.24;

contract Score {
    uint24[] score;                        Define a dynamic array

    function addScore(uint24 s) public returns(uint24[]) {
        score.push(s);
        return score;
                                           Will add to the array
    }

    function getLength() view public returns(uint) {
        return score.length;
    }

    function clearArray() public returns(uint24[]) {
        delete score;
        return score;
    }                                      Deletes the array
}
```

In dynamic arrays, you can now have access to the push member, which adds an element to the end of the array.

As you can see here, we have a function add score in the Score contract.

This adds a new score to the array.

Below this, we have a function get length, which gives us the number of elements in the array.

And at the end we have the clear array function.

To use this just type the delete keyword and the name of the array and it will delete all elements in the array and leave it blank.

Now that you are somewhat familiar with Remix, you will have the assignment to type those two contracts there.

Deploy each contract and play around with the arrays.

Try to add array elements to a dynamic array with the push member, retrieve the length of your array and delete the array.

Also, try to change the values of a fixed size array and retrieve elements by position as shown in the examples.

After that, continue to the next lecture.

Get FREE Video Lessons on Solidity at codingsrc.com/solidity

Memory vs Storage

Ok now in this lecture we are going to talk about where solidity stores our variables and how does it handle them.

And more specifically we are going to talk about the difference between memory and storage.

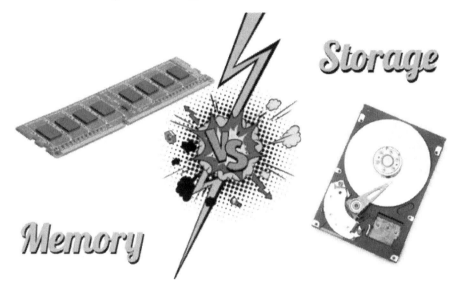

So... A contract's storage variables are the ones, which define your contract's state and are only changed by transaction calls.

Memory variables are temporary variables that exist only inside the calling function. They get wiped after the function exits and they are generally cheaper to use than storage variables.

So basically you should imagine storage and memory variables as the RAM and Hard Drive.

The memory uses variables for the current process or function and frees them after it is done using them.

And with storage you should imagine that we write a file on the hard drive and save it there.

Now... the state variables that we define are by default storage and the function arguments are by default memory.

Let's check this example contract now:

```
MEMORY VS STORAGE
pragma solidity ^0.4.24;

contract ChangeArrayValue {
    uint[20] public arr;            Storage by default

    function startChange() public {
        firstChange(arr);
        secondChange(arr);
    }                               Can be transformed to storage

    function firstChange(uint[20] storage x) internal {
        x[0] = 4;
    }

    function secondChange(uint[20] x) internal pure {
        x[0] = 3;
    }                   Memory by default,
}                       Makes a copy of the given variable
}
```

As you can see, we have a state variable array and 3 functions

We have a function called start change that calls two other functions.

The first function however, called first change has an explicitly defined storage variable as arguments.

And the second function called "second change" is with the default function arguments which is memory.

In both functions, we want to try to change the first element in the array.

What do you think we will get as a first element of the array after we run the function start change?

You can stop here and copy the contract to remix to test it out. It will be a great practice for you.

If you tested it in Remix, you would know that the answer is 4. But why is that?

This is because when we give a variable to a function, the function makes a copy of this variable and does all the operation with this copy.

After the function has finished it destroys the variables.

And if we define a function argument to be storage explicitly, we are saying that we want to do all operations to the variable that we give reference to.

Do not make a copy; use the storage variable that I gave you.

This is why the "firstChange" function makes changes to the array and the second seems to NOT make any changes whatsoever.

Now that you know a little bit more about memory and storage, let's continue to our next lecture.

Get FREE Video Lessons on Solidity at codingsrc.com/solidity

Mappings

In this lecture, we are going to talk about mappings in solidity

In solidity, mappings are referred to hash tables with the so-called key type and value type.

You can make an association with key value pairs in other programming languages.

Mappings are used to structure value types, such as booleans, integers, addresses, structs etc.

The most import thing is that the keys must be of the same type and the values must be of the same type.

So you can have keys of only addresses and values of only integers like here.

```solidity
pragma solidity ^0.4.24;

                          KeyType   Value Type
contract Bank {
    mapping(address => uint) public accounts;

    function deposit(uint money) public {
        accounts[msg.sender] += money;
    }

    function withdraw(uint money) public {
        accounts[msg.sender] -= money;
    }
}
```

Now as you can see we have a contract called Bank with a mapping called accounts.

We define our mapping with the keyword mapping and in brackets, we put the key type first then an arrow and the value type second.

After that the visibility and the name of the mapping.

As you can see, it is possible to mark mappings with public.

This will make solidity create a getter.

The key type will become a required parameter for the getter and it will return the value type.

You should also remember that **mappings can only use elementary types for keys.**

Elementary types are **address, uint, bytes, string and bool.**

However, I don't think you would want to use bool as a key as it only has two possible values.

Right below it we have two functions of deposit and withdraw

Here as you can see we get the value of the mapping as if it was an array.

We give the address of the person who is calling the function so only he can make a deposit to his account.

And with the withdraw we deduct money from the account of the sender as well.

Now let's see a simple token contract.

MAPPINGS

```solidity
pragma solidity ^0.4.24;

contract SimpleToken {
    address owner;
    mapping (address => uint256) public accounts;

    constructor(uint256 initialSupply) public {
        owner = msg.sender;
        accounts[owner] = initialSupply;
    }

    function transfer(address to, uint256 value) public {
        require(accounts[msg.sender] >= value);        // Check balance
        require(accounts[to] + value >= accounts[to]);
        accounts[msg.sender] -= value;
        accounts[to] += value;                          // Overflow check
    }
}
```
Subtract and add

Here as you can see we have defined mapping accounts with key address and value uint256.

In the constructor, we provide the initial supply of tokens and add them to the creators account.

Now below this we have defined a transfer function that can send the tokens to the desired address.

However first we check that we have enough tokens to transfer and after that, we check for overflow. (We will discuss those restrictions in later lectures)

Right after that, we do the transaction.

We subtract the amount from the owners account and add them to the given address.

The assignment for this lecture would be to copy this contract to Remix and build upon it.

Create a function that returns the balance of a certain account address.

Also we need a function that returns us the available tokens supply.

At the end, you can try to create a payable function that will receive ether and will send tokens to the sender based on a fixed exchange rate that you can come up with.

ASSIGNMENT SUMMARY:

1. Go ahead and copy the contracts and test them out in **https://remix.ethereum.org**

2. Create a function that **returns the balance of a certain account**

3. Create a function that returns the **available tokens supply**

4. Create a **payable function** that receives ether and it will send tokens to the sender.

After you have finished continue with the next lecture.

Structs

In this lecture, we are going to talk about **struct** types in solidity.

Now… Solidity gives us a way to define new types in the form of structs.

They are basically like objects with different types of characteristics inside.

Struct types can be used inside mappings and arrays and they can itself contain mappings and arrays.

A thing you should remember is that it is not possible for a struct to contain a member of its own type, although the struct itself can be the value type of a mapping member

Like in the example contract Bank here.

STRUCTS

```solidity
pragma solidity^0.4.24;

contract Bank {
    struct Account {
        address addr;
        uint amount;
    }

    Account public acc = Account({
        addr: 0x66ec542D55a86F2Fd0B0d9cB9f31bc20aC02477a,
        amount: 50
    });

    function addAmount(uint _addMoney) public {
        acc.amount += _addMoney;
    }
}
```

We have created a struct called account.

Inside we have the address and an unsigned integer for the amount.

Now that we have defined our new type of variable, we can initialize it.

Here we have defined a public account with the values this address and the amount of 50.

Now if you want to access a member of a struct you do that with dot and the name of the member you want to access.

We have defined a function **addAmount** that adds money to the amount of the account.

Now your job will be to copy the contract in solidity and test out how receive the struct type there when we call the account getter.

You should also try the addAmount function and add a withdraw function that will deduct money from the account.

If you want to take it to the next level, you should create one more account with a different address and create one more function called transfer.

The transfer function should have a **uint** that receives the money to transfer and should deduct the money from the first account and add them to the second.

Now stop here and go to remix to do you assignment and after that come back and continue with the lectures.

ASSIGNMENT SUMMARY:

1. Copy the contract and test it out in REMIX

2. Add amount to the account with the function "addAmount"

3. Create a function "withdraw" that deducts money from the account

4. Create one more Account

5. Create a function transfer that deducts money from first account and adds them to the second

Get FREE Video Lessons on Solidity at codingsrc.com/solidity

Error Handling & Restrictions

In this lecture, we are going to talk about error handling and exceptions in solidity.

Solidity uses state-reverting exceptions to handle errors.

When we have such exceptions all the changes will undo to the state of the current call.

We have three functions that can do that for us. **Assert, require and revert**.

Let's first look at the most common way to restrict condition - the function require.

Require is mostly used to validate user input and external contract responses.

Let's check our example contract here:

REQUIRE CONDITIONS

```solidity
pragma solidity ^0.4.24;
contract Bank {
    mapping(address => uint) public accounts;

    function deposit() public payable {
        require(accounts[msg.sender] + msg.value >=
accounts[msg.sender], "Overflow error");
        accounts[msg.sender] += msg.value;
    }
```

> Checks for overflow of **user input**

```solidity
    function withdraw(uint money) public {
        require(money <= accounts[msg.sender]);
        accounts[msg.sender] -= money;
    }
}
```

> Will **not allow user** to withdraw more than what he has

We have the contract Bank with the deposit and withdraw function as in the previous lectures.

However, what happens if the user wants to deposit more than the max value of **uint256**?

That is right. The number **overflows**. We have mentioned this in the lecture about variables.

This is why we would want to restrict our user inputs to be valid.

In the **first function**, we make sure that whenever we try to add money to the account the amount actually increases.

This require function will prevent from overflow and if the condition is not met, it will revert all of the remaining gas to the sender as well as the ether sent with the transaction.

As you can see, we can also provide an error message that the caller can receive if the condition is not met.

I our case this is "Overflow error".

In the **second function** we just want to make sure that the money that we want to withdraw are less or equal to the accounts balance.

This way we will not withdraw more money then what we have in the account and underflow our balance to a ridiculously large number.

Now let's take a look at the other way that we can do that - the function revert:

REVERT CONDITIONS

```
contract Bank {
    mapping(address => uint) public accounts;

    function deposit() public payable {
      if(accounts[msg.sender] + msg.value >=
accounts[msg.sender]) {
        revert("Overflow error");        Provides explanation
        }
        accounts[msg.sender] += money;
    }

    function withdraw(uint money) public {
        if(money <= accounts[msg.sender]){
          //can have more if statements
                                          Can be used for
          revert();                       complex if checks
        }
        accounts[msg.sender] -= money;
    }
}
```

The revert works basically the same as the require function, however, it can be used as a flag when a more complex if conditions are met.

In the require function you had only one line that you can put your condition in.

With a revert you can make some complex checks with if else statements and when you come to the revert function it will make the transaction go back to the previous state.

There is also no change in the fact that revert as well as require refunds all of the remaining gas.

NOW… Let's take a look at the assert function example.

ASSERT CONDITIONS

```solidity
pragma solidity^0.4.24;

contract Math {

function add(uint256 a, uint256 b) internal pure returns (uint) {
    c = a + b;
    assert(c >= a);
    return c;
}

function multiply(uint256 a, uint256 b) internal pure returns (uint) {
    if (a == 0) {
        return 0;
    }
    c = a * b;
    assert(c / a == b);
    return c;
}
}
```

> Will check for overflow in **internal** invariants

> Will check for overflow in **internal** invariants

Here we have a sample contract Math that has two functions…. Add and multiply.

As per the documentation, the assert function should only be used to test for internal errors, and to check invariants

As you can see our functions here are internal and we prevent with the assert function an overflow of our numbers.

If we give the function add a bigger number then the max value of uint256, the assert will invalidate the transaction.

However, you should remember that assert will use all of the remaining gas.

You should use assert to avoid conditions which should never, ever be possible.

One thing that you should remember is that assert validates state after making changes.

Now here I have made for you a little cheat sheet that you can look at for better understanding what are all the differences between the functions.

What is the difference?

revert();
- Same as require();
- Will undo all the changes you had made in blockchain.
- **if/else** logic flow. For complex checks.
- can be used to flag an error and revert the current call
- Refunds remaining gas.

require();
- Validate user inputs
- Validate the response from an external contract
- ie. use require(external.send(amount))
- Validate state conditions prior to executing state changing operations, for example in an owned contract situation
- Generally, you should use require more often,
- Generally, it will be used towards the beginning of a function.

assert();
- check for overflow/underflow
- check invariants
- validate contract state *after* making changes
- avoid conditions which should never, ever be possible.
- Generally, you should use assert less often
- Generally, it will be use towards the end of your function.

Your assignment for this lecture would be to go back to the contracts you have made by now and think about the restrictions you can make you user inputs and numbers.

Are there any functions that might overflow or underflow a number, or would you want this function to be accessible only by the owner of the contract?

Use the appropriate function to restrict that from happening and after that continue to the next lecture.

Get FREE Video Lessons on Solidity at codingsrc.com/solidity

Libraries

In this lecture, we are going to talk about libraries and their function.

In Solidity, a library is a different type of contract, that doesn't have any storage and cannot hold ether.

As they don't have storage, they don't have state variables as well and cannot inherit or be inherited.

Libraries are basically a piece of code that can be attached to a variable and use the functions predefined as members of the given type.

We define a library with the keyword library and its reference name after that.

Now here we have a very popular library called SafeMath.

LIBRARY

Library for math operations that prevents overflow/underflow

```
pragma solidity ^0.4.24;

library SafeMath {
    function mul(uint256 a, uint256 b) internal pure returns (uint256) {
        uint256 c = a * b;
        assert(a == 0 || c / a == b);
        return c;
    }

    function div(uint256 a, uint256 b) internal pure returns (uint256) {
        // assert(b > 0); // Solidity automatically throws when dividing by 0
        uint256 c = a / b;
        // assert(a == b * c + a % b); // There is no case in which this doesn't hold
        return c;
    }

    function sub(uint256 a, uint256 b) internal pure returns (uint256) {
        assert(b <= a);
        return a - b;
    }

    function add(uint256 a, uint256 b) internal pure returns (uint256) {
        uint256 c = a + b;
        assert(c >= a);
        return c;
    }
}
```

This library prevents math operations to overflow or underflow the numbers.

As you can see here, we have multiplication, division, subtraction and addition.

However, how do we use a library?

Let's see how we can use this in our solidity contract here.

```solidity
LIBRARY USAGE                    Import the library from GitHub.com
pragma solidity ^0.4.24;
import "github.com/OpenZeppelin/
zeppelin-solidity/contracts/math/SafeMath.sol";

contract Bank {
    mapping(address => uint) public accounts;
    using SafeMath for uint256;      Define for what you use SafeMath

    function deposit() public payable {
        require(accounts[msg.sender] + msg.value >= accounts[msg.sender],
"Overflow error");
        accounts[msg.sender] = accounts[msg.sender].add(msg.value);
    }
                                 .add member makes addition

    function withdraw(uint money) public {
        require(money <= accounts[msg.sender]);
        accounts[msg.sender] = accounts[msg.sender].sub(money);
    }
}
```

As you can see, we can import the library from GitHub directly.

Just use import, the name of the library and the link to the library file.

You can also import a library as a local file by providing the destination to the file.

After that, we define that we are going to attach this library to uint256 variable types.

And now we have access to all the functions in the library as members of the variables uint256.

Although in the library we needed two arguments in the function, the variable that we use this on is accepted as the first argument, and the second argument is the one in the brackets.

The same applies to the subtraction function over here.

Now you know how a library is used in solidity.

To test it out import the safe math library from GitHub inside a previous contract you have made.

Attach the SafeMath to the uint256 variables and change all the math operations to go through the library functions as shown in the example.

This will prevent the overflow and underflow of your numbers.

After you finish go to the next lecture.

Get FREE Video Lessons on Solidity at codingsrc.com/solidity

Modifiers

Now we are going to talk about modifiers.

In Solidity, we can create our own modifiers, which can change the behavior- of functions just by adding the modifier keyword to the function.

For example, they can automatically check a condition prior to executing a function.

```
MODIFIER

pragma solidity ^0.4.24;

contract Purchase {                    Define your own
    address public seller;             modifier

    modifier onlySeller { // Modifier
        require(msg.sender == seller);
        _;                             Usually for restrictions
    }
         Placeholder for the rest of the code

    function abort() public onlySeller { // Modifier usage
        // ...
    }
}
```

Now in this sample contract we have defined a modifier called onlySeller.

We define that with the keyword modifier and the name of the modifier we want to create.

Inside the curly brackets we define what we want the function to check or do whenever we have this modifier.

Usually modifiers are used for restriction to save us time from writing in every function a require line like this.

However, they can be used for more than that.

Now after the lines of code that we want to execute in the function we have placed an underscore and semicolon.

This is like a placeholder for the code of the function.

However, don't be confused.

You can have the underscore first and after that, some code.

Alternatively, you can have some code, the placeholder and after that, some code too.

Now we apply the modifier as other modifiers of a function like here.

This modifier will always check if the user is the seller whenever it is applied to a function and it will revert if it is not.

Now let's look at another example.

MODIFIER

```solidity
pragma solidity ^0.4.24;

contract owned {
    constructor() public { owner = msg.sender; }
    address owner;

    modifier onlyOwner {        ─── Define your own modifier
        require(msg.sender == owner);
        _;
    }
}
                                    Modifiers are inheritable
contract mortal is owned {          properties of contracts

    function close() public onlyOwner {
        selfdestruct(owner);
    }                               Destroys the contract
}
```

One thing that you need to keep in mind is that modifiers are inheritable properties of contracts and may be overridden by derived contracts.

This means that if you have a contract with modifiers and another contract inherits this contract you will be able to access the modifiers and use them there, as in the example.

Here we have two contracts owned and mortal and the mortal contract inherits the owned contract.

This means that in the mortal contract we can use the modifier onlyOwner without defining it.

Now your assignment will be to go through your previous contracts that you applied your restriction.

Think about where you can apply a restriction of onlyOwner and create a modifier for that.

After that apply the modifier to the functions that need to be executed only by the owner.

After you have finished your assignment, continue to the next lecture.

Get FREE Video Lessons on Solidity at codingsrc.com/solidity

Global Variables

In this lecture, we are going to go through the global variables that we have in solidity.

There are a lot of variables that are predefined and we can use them as they are,

First, we are going to take a look at the ether units that we have.

If you don't know, Ethereum has a metric system of denominations used as units of ether.

Each denomination has its own unique name but the smallest denomination aka base unit of ether is called Wei.

There are many different units however in solidity we have only **finney szabo**, **ether** and **wei** that we can use.

Here you can see the conversion rate for them.

```
ETHER UNITS
1 ether = 1000 finney
1 ether = 1,000,000 szabo
1 ether = 1,000,000,000,000,000,000 wei

1 finney = 0.001 ether
1 finney = 1000 szabo
1 finney = 1,000,000,000,000,000 wei

1 szabo = 0.000001 ether
1 szabo = 0.001 finney
1 szabo = 1,000,000,000,000 wei
```

Now... we also have some time units that we can use.

Here is a list of the time units in solidity.

We have seconds, minutes, hours days and weeks. We used to have years as well but it became deprecated because not every year has 365 days.

We also have block and transaction properties as global variables.

- block.blockhash(uint blockNumber) returns (bytes32): hash of the given block - only works for 256 most recent, excluding current, blocks - deprecated in version 0.4.22 and replaced by blockhash(uint blockNumber).
- block.coinbase (address): current block miner's address
- block.difficulty (uint): current block difficulty
- block.gaslimit (uint): current block gaslimit
- block.number (uint): current block number
- block.timestamp (uint): current block timestamp as seconds since unix epoch
- gasleft() returns (uint256): remaining gas
- msg.data (bytes): complete calldata
- msg.gas (uint): remaining gas - deprecated in version 0.4.21 and to be replaced by gasleft()
- msg.sender (address): sender of the message (current call)
- msg.sig (bytes4): first four bytes of the calldata (i.e. function identifier)
- msg.value (uint): number of wei sent with the message
- now (uint): current block timestamp (alias for block.timestamp)
- tx.gasprice (uint): gas price of the transaction
- tx.origin (address): sender of the transaction (full call chain)

As you can see, we have 3 main variables - **block**, **msg** and **tx**

From the block variable, we have members as **blockhash**, **coinbase**, **difficulty**, **gaslimit**, **number** and **timestamp**.

Each has an explicit explanation here, however, the most used variables the timestamp which returns the time now - the same as the now variable, which is an alias.

For the message variable, the most important are the msg.sender, which returns the sender of the message as address, and the **msg.value**, which returns the number of **wei** that send with the call.

We also have cryptographic and math functions integrated in Solidity:

- `addmod(uint x, uint y, uint k) returns (uint):`
  compute (x + y) % k where the addition is performed with arbitrary precision and does not wrap around at 2**256. Assert that k != 0 starting from version 0.5.0.
- `mulmod(uint x, uint y, uint k) returns (uint):`
  compute (x * y) % k where the multiplication is performed with arbitrary precision and does not wrap around at 2**256. Assert that k != 0 starting from version 0.5.0.
- `keccak256(...) returns (bytes32):`
  compute the Ethereum-SHA-3 (Keccak-256) hash of the (tightly packed) arguments
- `sha256(...) returns (bytes32):`
  compute the SHA-256 hash of the (tightly packed) arguments
- `sha3(...) returns (bytes32):`
  alias to keccak256
- `ripemd160(...) returns (bytes20):`
  compute RIPEMD-160 hash of the (tightly packed) arguments
- `ecrecover(bytes32 hash, uint8 v, bytes32 r, bytes32 s) returns (address):`
  recover the address associated with the public key from elliptic curve signature or return zero on error (example usage)

We have the sha3, which is the same as keccak256 hash, sha256 and ripemd160, that can encrypt our inputs.

We also have math functions like **addmod** and **mulmod** that returns the modulo operation for addition of two numbers and the multiplication of the numbers respectively.

And last but not least, we have contract related global variables.

CONTRACT RELATED

```
this (current contract's type):
the current contract, explicitly
convertible to Address

selfdestruct(address recipient):
destroy the current contract, sending
its funds to the given Address

suicide(address recipient):
deprecated alias to selfdestruct
```

We have the **this** keyword which is related to the current contract and is explicitly convertible to address.

We also have **selfdestruct**, which destroys the current contract and sends its funds to the given address.

Suicide is a deprecated alias for **selfdestruct**.

So now, you have a brief look at the global variables that we can have.

Now let's continue with our next lecture.

Get FREE Video Lessons on Solidity at codingsrc.com/solidity

Abstract Contracts, Inheritance & Interfaces

Now we are going to talk about abstract contracts, inheritance and interfaces in solidity

If you have no prior knowledge of abstract classes with other programming languages, we use them to extract common features between contracts that we have so we won't have repetitive code.

This will help us a lot if we want to change something that all contracts have in common and we will only change it once in the abstract contract and it will apply to the derivative contracts as well.

The best way to explain this is to take a look at this example:

ABSTRACT CONTRACT

```
pragma solidity ^0.4.24;

contract Animal {
    string public breed;
    uint public age;              Can define default variables.
    uint public weight;

    constructor() public {
        age = 1;                  Can define default constructor
        weight = 1;
    }

    function sleep() pure public returns (string) {return Zzzz...";}

    function eat() pure public returns (string) {return "Nom nom..";}

    function talk() pure public returns (string);
}
```

One function that **lacks implementation makes the contract abstract**

Here we have a abstract contract animal that has defined public variables breed, age and weight.

We have also created a default constructor which if we do not override we have our age of 1 and weight of 1.

We also have 2 implemented functions sleep and eat and one not implemented function called talk.

Contracts are marked as abstract when at least one of their functions lacks an implementation as in our example.

Note that the function talk in the abstract contract is terminated by semicolon.

It is a way for the designer of the abstract contract to say, "Any child of mine must implement these functions".

ABSTRACT CONTRACT

```solidity
pragma solidity ^0.4.24;

contract Animal {
    string public breed;
    uint public age;
    uint public weight;

    constructor() public {
        age = 1;
        weight = 1;
    }

    function sleep() pure public returns (string) {return Zzzz...";}

    function eat() pure public returns (string) {return "Nom nom..";}

    function talk() pure public returns (string);
}
```

Can define **default variables.**

Can define **default constructor**

One function that **lacks implementation makes the contract abstract**

Now the contracts Cat and Dog implement the abstract contract with the keyword **'is'** and they inherit the implemented functions sleep, eat, and are obligated to override the talk function.

We have also overridden the constructor and the variables that define the breed, age and weight.

Now let's look what is the difference between abstract contracts and interfaces.

```solidity
pragma solidity ^0.4.11;

interface Token {

    function transfer(address recipient,
uint amount) public;

    function balanceOf(address _owner)
constant returns (uint256 balance);

}
```

1. Cannot inherit other contracts or interfaces.
2. Cannot have functions with implementation
3. Cannot define constructor.
4. Cannot define variables.
5. Cannot define structs.
6. Cannot define enums.

We defined them with the keyword interface instead of contract and after that we give the reference name.

We also have some restrictions like that they cannot inherit other contracts or interfaces.

They can't have functions with implementations or a defined constructor.

Also we can NOT define variables, structs and enums in interfaces.

Basically you should imagine an interface as a skeleton of our contracts.

We define what kind of functions we need to have in the contracts that inherit the interface.

When a contract inherits an interface, it needs to implement all of its functions.

Now as you know the 'is' keyword means that our contract inherits an interface or a contract.

Solidity supports multiple inheritance.

INTERFACES

```solidity
contract PriceFeed is owned, mortal, named("GoldFeed") {
    function updateInfo(uint newInfo) public {
        if (msg.sender == owner) info = newInfo;
    }

    function get() public view returns(uint r) { return
info; }

    uint info;
}
```

When a contract inherits multiple contracts, only a single contract is created on the blockchain, and the code from all the base contracts is copied into the created contract.

When you want to inherit multiple contracts or interfaces, you need to separate them by comma.

Also as in this example, we have a contract that inherits multiple contracts.

If one of the constructors of the contracts receives arguments, it needs to be specified in the header as you can see here.

Now we know more about abstract contracts, interfaces and inheritance.

Let's continue to the next lecture.

Get FREE Video Lessons on Solidity at codingsrc.com/solidity

Events

In this lecture, we are going to talk about events.

Events are a great way to tell our decentralized application vie JavaScript callbacks that something has happened.

We can as well send information alongside the event.

To do that we first need to predefine our event with the keyword event and after that the reference name of the event.

```
EVENTS CONTRACT SIDE

pragma solidity ^0.4.24;

contract SmartExchange {
    event Deposit(address from, bytes32 to, uint indexed  value);
    event Transfer(bytes32 from, address to, uint indexed value);

    function deposit(bytes32 to) payable public {
        emit Deposit(msg.sender, to, msg.value);
    }

    function transfer(bytes32 from, address to, uint value) payable
public{
        to.transfer(value);
        emit Transfer(from, to, value);
    }
}
```

Event definition — *Can receive indexed attribute*

Emitting our event

Inside the brackets, we specify which variables we want to send to our DApp whenever the DApp catches the event.

We can also specify up to three variables with the keyword indexed which will cause the respective arguments to be searched for.

This way it will be possible to filter for specific values of indexed arguments in the user interface.

Now when we want to emit our event we use the emit keyword and the reference name of the specific event.

And inside the brackets we give the desired parameters we want to pass to our UI.

In the JavaScript side of our application we are going to be listening to those events and catch them and receive the arguments that we have passed.

We are going to go through this in more details in the next section of our course.

For now we can test if our events are working correctly if we copy this contract inside remix and run the functions.

So let's go to remix and paste this contract and compile it.

Now let's copy another ether wallet address from the dropdown menu here.

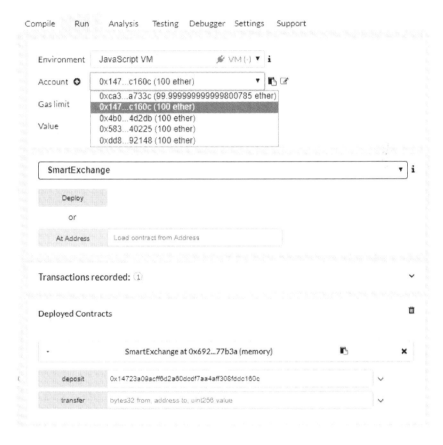

And now let's deposit some amount to that account and see what we will receive.

Let's enter 100 weis and paste the wallet address and click deposit.

Now as you can see we have our transaction successfully executed and we have a new table row called logs.

Here you can see all the events we had emitted during our transaction and their details.

decoded output	{}
logs	[
	{
	"from": "0x602a70d2e424a56d2c6c27aa97d1a86395877b3a",
	"topic": "0x19dacbf83c5de6e58e14cbf7bcae5c15eca2eedecf1c66fbca92ae4d351bea
	ef",
	"event": "Deposit",
	"args": {
	"0": "0x14723A89ACFf6D2A60DcdF7aA4AFf308FDDC160C",
	"1": "0x14723a09acff6d2a60dcdf7aa4aff308fddc16ec000000000000000000
	e00000",
	"2": "100",
	"from": "0x14723A89ACFf6D2A60DcdF7aA4AFf308FDDC160C",
	"to": "0x14723a09acff6d2a60dcdf7aa4aff308fddc16ec0000000000000000000
	0000000",
	"value": "100",
	"length": 3
	}
	}
	]
value	100 wei

Here you can see the contract from which we have emitted the event and the topic is the event with its arguments encrypted with sha3.

Now in this case we have only one event emitted called deposit.

However, if we had multiple events here, they will be separated with comma and be presented here like a JSON array.

As you can see, we have our name of the event and the arguments inside which are accessible by name or by the position.

And at the end we have length which gives us the number of arguments inside the event.

Now you know the basics of events and what we can do from the contracts side of a DApp.

In the future lecture we are going to discuss in more details how we can catch those events with the arguments that they have and display them in our decentralized applications.

Now for an assignment, you will have to copy this contract and play around with it in remix and take a look at the log row that we have when we rise an event.

You will need to create a new simple event and emit it inside the deposit function.

This way you will be able to see how you will get multiple events in the log row.

Conclusion

Thank you again for buying this book!

I hope this book was able to help you to get the basics of Solidity In place.

The next step is to sign up for our free video course offer in this book or go and get the full video course on Udemy with our special discount coupon: **KD876SOL**

GET HERE:

https://www.udemy.com/solidity-smart-contracts-build-dapps-in-ethereum-blockchain/?couponCode=KD878SOL

Here is some more info about the full course:

For the past couple of years there hasn't been a bigger brake through in the IT world than the one that the **Blockchain technology** has made. The extremely fast growth of the industry, market and the technology itself leads to enormous **shortage of programmers** that truly understand the blockchain. Along with the blockchain smart contracts have emerged and with them - **Solidity**.

The idea of this course if to give you the easiest and best practices in becoming a blockchain developer. We will be focusing on the **smart contracts** development with **Solidity** in the **Ethereum ecosystem.**

You will learn to create your first smart contracts in the Ethereum blockchain even if you are a complete beginner and you know nothing about programming or Solidity.

I will show you the **online IDE Remix** to create your first smart contracts and we will go through all the features that **Solidity** provides us as a **programming language.**

You will also be able to set up your environment to start coding with Solidity on your local machine. I will show you what settings and configurations I used to set up my **VSCode** and **how to successfully install Truffle on Windows.**

After that I will teach you the basics of the **Truffle Framework** and how to make it work with **Ganache** as your own **private Ethereum blockchain network.**

We will also test out our Solidity smart contracts behavior with **unit testing with Chai and Mocha.** If you are a serious developer you need to know that your code is working the way you expect it does.

When you are finished you will be able to create your own **first decentralized application** with **Solidity and Truffle**.

While other courses are filled in with unnecessary information that make them hard to navigate through and leave you confused, this course will take you step by step **from a complete beginner to a master of Solidity** and smart contracts creation in the Ethereum ecosystem.

In this course:

- We'll learn the essentials of the **Ethereum blockchain**. How to make and **protect our wallets** as well as mastering **Metamask** as our main Ethereum wallet in the creation of our **smart contracts.**

- We will go through the **basic and advanced concepts of the Solidity language.** We learn in depth how you can build your own smart contracts and **test them out instantly in Remix.**

- I will teach you how to use **Metamask as your Ethereum wallet** and I will give you security advice that will **keep your crypto assets secure.**

- We will also go through how you can **develop your own DApp** with Solidity and the **Truffle Framework + Ganache** as your virtual blockchain and the right way to set up your development environment.

- We will learn the **essentials in DApp development with Solidity** as well as unit testing of our smart contracts, so we can make sure our code behaves the way we expect.

- **You will have assignments** that will help you out understand the material better with actual practice and not only passive consumption. After you finish this course **you will fall in love with Solidity, Ethereum ecosystem and the smart contracts creation.**

GET HERE:

https://www.udemy.com/solidity-smart-contracts-build-dapps-in-ethereum-blockchain/?couponCode=KD878SOL

Finally, if you enjoyed this book, then I'd like to ask you for a favor, would you be kind enough to **leave a review on the website you bought it from**. It'd be greatly appreciated and would help a lot.

Thank you and good luck!

41020772R00053

Made in the USA
San Bernardino, CA
30 June 2019